The Tree of Love

A Simple Plan for Women to Change the World

BY JAN BUBBENMOYER

Copyright © 2011 Jan Bubbenmoyer

All rights reserved.

ISBN: 0615440428

ISBN-13: 9780615440422

Library of Congress Control Number: 2011901278

Mary —
Do everything with love —

xxxooo
Jan

Woman is the heart of the home. Let us pray that we realize the reason for our existence; to love and be loved and through this love, become instruments of peace in the world.

Mother Teresa

Table of Contents

Dedication–3

Preface–5

The Tree of Love–7

The First Branch—Start with Family–11

The Second Branch—Spread the Word–17

The Third Branch—Branching Out–25

What We Need to Change–31

Lack of Love and Care, Loneliness, Hunger

What We Can Do–41

Love, Smile, Make a Loving Home,

Bring Joy, Be Grateful, Nurture, Care,

Pray for Guidance, Give Thanks

Inspiration–67

Tree of Love Pledge–78

Food for Thought–80

Charities–86

Tree of Love Workbook Pages–89

Dedication

For Mother Teresa of Calcutta
and the Missionaries of Charity

May we be brave enough
to follow your example

May we be loving enough to heal the broken
spirits of those who are sad and lonely

May we use every gift God has given us for the
benefit of all people
and
May you, Mother, always be with us
to guide and inspire.

Preface

No one is more surprised by the fact that I have written this book than me.

It was not part of my plans. It was not something I had floating around in my mind. I was in the process of writing a book of essays about some humorous and some serious aspects of life. That's what I was thinking about.

One night, I picked up a copy of Mother Teresa's little book, *In the Heart of the World*, from my night stand. I had never even looked at it before, although I'd had it for several years. I thought it would be interesting reading and I could finish it during my bath.

I began reading.
"In the silence of the heart God speaks.
If you face God in prayer and silence, God will speak to you.
Then you will know that you are nothing.
It is only when you realize your nothingness, your emptiness, that God can fill you with Himself."
I began to cry.

Everything she said in that book spoke to my heart in a way I had never before experienced. I was so profoundly affected that the next day I sat down at the computer and began to write this book. Actually, the book seemed to write itself. I feel as though I was the messenger.

PREFACE

I suppose it doesn't matter how I got the message. What is important is that I deliver it. Mother once said,
"If you want a message of love to be heard, it has to be sent out."
This is our call to love. It's our chance to change the world. I believe that with all my heart. I hope you want to be a part of it as much as I do.

The Tree of Love

Women are the ones who will save the world, if it is to be saved. Our capacity for nurture, care, compassion and love is limitless. In this realm, no one is more capable. I truly believe that we can do this by simply being who we are, by coming together and creating a new level of love and caring in our world.

No one can "out love" the heart of a woman.

If you look at the life of Mother Teresa and see all she accomplished with the Sisters of Charity, think about how much we could accomplish with all the women in the world, working together to spread love, compassion, peace, and caring.

We don't need to run countries to do this. It's better that we don't. We can work behind the scenes, starting with our families and other people we know,
expanding to local charities and people we don't know, branch out even farther and then start connecting all the little branches until we have a "tree of love" that supports the emotional and physical needs of the indigent, the lonely, and the disenfranchised throughout the world.

THE TREE OF LOVE

We do all we can, whenever we can, for whomever we can, and we encourage all the women we know to do the same. The strength and love of all women on the planet coming together would be so powerful that we could overcome anything.
Our tree will spread its branches and leaves over the world so that all people will be protected in the shade of God's love, compassion, and peace.

"Let us not be satisfied with giving money. Money is not enough. They need your hearts to love them."

Mother Teresa

The Tree of Love is more than a plan.
It's a philosophy.

Eventually, we will incorporate it into our daily lives. As it becomes a part of us, we will change even more lives with our love and compassion.

*It is easy to love people far away,
very easy to think of hungry people in India.
You must first see that there is love
at home and at your next door
neighbors and on the street and in the town
where you live. Only then do you go
beyond to the outside world"*

Mother Teresa

The Tree of Love Plan

FIRST BRANCH

Start with Family

*"What can you do to promote world peace?
Go home and love your family."*

Mother Teresa

First Branch

Start with your own family and friends

Plant the seeds of love, caring, and compassion, and make sure they are growing in your own life before you venture out to help the world.

Your family needs this foundation of your love. If you can't help the people you love best, how will you help others?
This includes your
extended family of in-laws, elderly relatives, and older family friends.

- Are any of your friends ill or going through a difficult time?
- Are your own children hungry for some time with you in which they feel your love for them?
- Does your husband need more encouragement or support or tenderness from you?
- Do you know of any friends or family in the hospital? Is there something you can do for their family, such as cook a meal or invite them to dinner one night?

- Perhaps a phone call or a visit to someone you know is hurting or has just lost a loved one could help.
- Is someone you know going through a divorce and in need of emotional support or just a dinner with a friend?

You need to think about people in your life and be able to assess their circumstances to truly know if anyone needs your help.

Putting the Plan to Work

FIRST BRANCH CHECKLIST

- Make a list of family and friends.
- Decide what more you can do for each of these loved ones in terms of loving and caring for them.
- Formulate your plan for each one, and write it down.
- Begin putting your plan to work.
- Start loving, nurturing, and caring more for those you love.

EXAMPLE

For your children, it could be saying "I love you"
more often,
being playful with them, laughing more.
They will notice your efforts and respond with
appreciation.
They will feel more loved.
You will feel more loving.

Even if you write a letter for someone who can't see, or if you just sit and listen or take in the mail for him or her, or bring a flower to brighten the day or wash clothes or clean the house- small things; God sees everything as great"

Mother Teresa

Tree of Love Plan

SECOND BRANCH

Spread the Word

Spread the word!

Have a potluck dinner for your friends.
Just invite five women—that's all.
Pick the five you believe would be most effective or most interested in participating in the project.
Tell them how important it is that they come. Let them know that their presence could help change the world—as crazy as it sounds!

When they arrive, share the concept of the project with them.
Assist them in formulating a list of people in their lives who could use extra love and care.

Help them determine what people on the list may need special attention. This may be difficult for them to see at first because we like to believe we
are doing our best with everyone at all times. But sometimes taking a fresh approach can produce amazing results for our families.

Explain to them what specific measures you have taken to change the lives of your loved ones and friends. Tell them what's working and what kind of a impact it's having.

SECOND BRANCH

When they are confident that the project is working in their lives and the lives of people closest to them, it's time for them to host

a Tree of Love Meeting

with five women of their choosing.
They should commit to having the meeting within a month. This keeps everything on a regular schedule, and people can't get lazy about it.

And so it goes ...

Each woman sponsors a group of five, and those five women sponsor a group of five, and we pass it on, sharing our successes and ideas and making sure that all the people in our circle are being cared for to the best of our ability.

*Each participant sponsors one group of five and each woman hosts just one meeting.

The Power of Five

If we start with five women at a meeting,
and each one sponsors a group of five,
and that group sponsors five more, and so on ... within one
year we will have 48 million women making a difference in
this world!

Month 1: 5 women
Month 2: 25 women
Month 3: 125 women
Month 4: 625 women
Month 5: 3,125 women
Month 6: 15,625 women
Month 7: 78,125 women
Month 8: 390,625 women
Month 9: 9,765,625 women
Month 12: 48,828,125 women

Spread the Word

SECOND BRANCH CHECKLIST

When you see that the plan for your loved ones is working in your life, then it's time to:

- Spread the word. Invite five like-minded women to a potluck dinner at your house.
- At the meeting, share with them the concept of the "Tree of Love."
- Tell them what you've been doing and how it's working.
- Help them devise a plan for their loved ones and closest friends.
- Have them agree to host their own "Tree of Love" meeting within a month, asking five of their like-minded friends, and begin to pass on the message.

Agree to be available for each one of your five friends if they want or need to talk or get additional information before they host their own meeting.

SECOND BRANCH

It's important to keep this process moving and have everyone understand what they're doing and agree to pass it on.

The Tree of Love Plan

THIRD BRANCH

Branching Out

Let us be very sincere in our dealings with each other and have the courage to accept each other as we are. Do not be surprised at each other's failures- rather see and find in each other the good. For each one of us is created in the image of God."

Mother Teresa

Branching Out

THIRD BRANCH

When you have completed the first two steps of the plan, the *third step is to:*

Research all the charitable organizations in your area.

After you have looked at what they do, who they serve, and how they serve, you must decide where you feel you could be most helpful.

Find out if there is someone in your church or neighborhood who needs help. Then begin making a difference in the lives of those who need your care.

Here is the staggering reality of the results we could produce:
If every woman in the project volunteers only one hour per week, we will have increased the number of volunteer hours by
<u>48 million hours per week after just one year.</u>

THIRD BRANCH

If every woman who has committed to the Tree of Love plan touches and changes the lives of only five people, including members of her family, through love and caring; then we will have made a difference in the lives of <u>over 240 million people in one year</u>!
How many times in your life have you been offered an opportunity to participate in something that could change the world?

Third Branch

CHECKLIST
BRANCHING OUT

- Find out about local charities.
- Decide which one feels closest to your heart and your goal.
- *Volunteer when and where you can.*
- Begin working in your community with your chosen charity and put your philosophy of love, compassion, and caring to work for the people you are serving through the charity.
- Look around every day and see the need, wherever it may be:

Then do something!

*"Deliver me, Lord, from:
the desire to be honored,
the desire to be praised,
the desire to be preferred,
the desire to be approved."*

Mother Teresa

THE TREE OF LOVE

What we need to change

"Loneliness—the worst poverty there is."

Mother Teresa

Loneliness

Our world is filled with the loneliness that comes
with hardship.
There is war, famine, disease, poverty, and lack of love.
There are so many horrors.
The quietest and least noticeable of these horrors is loneliness.
When people are alone in the world, they have no joy,
no hope, and no love in their lives. It robs their spirit of
happiness, and their bodies can wither as well.

Imagine not being able to have the comfort of a human
touch or hear an encouraging word from someone who
cares about you.
Can you imagine that?
If you can, then do something caring for a poor soul who is
drowning in loneliness.

Go to visit, sit, talk, and hold that person's hand. Let them know
that they are not alone. Let them feel important and cared for.
Little things can transform their lives and your life in the process.

*This is a form of poverty you can do something about.
It will cost you nothing but some of your time, and in
return it will enrich your spirit, too.*

"Only God's love can truly fill an empty heart."

Mother Teresa

Loss

There are so many kinds of loss in this world.

Loss of a loved one
Loss of employment
Loss of a home
Loss of hope
Loss of one's health

These are all life-changing losses.
People withdraw from the world because they cannot find a way to deal with the enormity of the situation.
When people suffer from loss, they become depressed and can drift away from the world and the people in their lives.
This may not truly be what they want, but they simply cannot a find a way to deal with anything,
so they withdraw.
If this is the case, we may be able to help.

We can visit, talk with the person, and find out how we might help with their circumstances. We may need to enlist other friends and family members.

If they are elderly and need to socialize,
you could find a senior center for them and arrange their transportation.

Maybe all they need is an encouraging word and a visit
during the week.
Perhaps they would prefer to speak to others who have
experienced a loss.
There are groups they could join.
Find those groups and help them get signed up.

If someone has lost a job, we can help by assisting them in
creating a resumé and looking into opportunities for them.
If their health has been bad, we can take them to an
appointment or bring them food at home.

Think about ways in which you can help, no matter
what the circumstances.
There is always something that can be done.
You may have to work with their relatives and other
friends, but a situation can always be made better
by love and care.

Lack of Love and Caring

So many people suffer from lack of love and care.
There are people who are estranged from their families.
There are those who have lost a loved one or spouse.
There are those who are physically and mentally disabled.
Usually, the poorest are the most affected. They have the
fewest resources, especially in rural areas.

Many programs and volunteers that
would be available in larger municipal areas may be
unknown to many of these people. At the same time, these
people may be unknown to anyone in the system who
could potentially help them.

*These are people we need to find with our network of
women. The souls who are truly alone and without
love and care are the people we must seek out. They
will benefit greatly from a little kindness and care.*

"Being unwanted, unloved, uncared for, forgotten by everybody; I think that is a much greater hunger, a much greater poverty than the person who has nothing to eat."

Mother Teresa

Hunger

There is physical hunger and hunger of the spirit.
Both must be conquered, because they both destroy lives.
World hunger is a huge problem. It will not be eradicated
overnight—perhaps not even in our lifetime.
But we can make progress.

We can commit to helping when and where
we see the need.
If there are millions of us and we all do only small things,
the results could be staggering.

That's why this plan can be so powerful. There are so many of us, and we are working together to achieve the same goal. This wouldn't be possible if we were all doing small things on our own.

Everyone yearns for love and understanding. Every time we feed a body, let us also commit to feeding their soul with our love and care.

- During the year, have your children bake cookies and take them to a homeless shelter.
- Head a clothing drive and take blankets and coats to a shelter.

- Invite a lonely neighbor or an elderly person with no family to share one of your Holiday dinners.
- Make sure you take the children to volunteer at a shelter or soup kitchen.
- Sponsor a neighborhood food drive and deliver to a local food bank.

We can change the world. Let us begin!

WORDS OF WISDOM

"Never worry about numbers.
Help one person at a time and always start with
the person nearest you."

"None of us can do great things, but we can do small
things with great love."

"I can do things you cannot, you can do things I cannot;
together we can do great things."

Mother Teresa

THE TREE OF LOVE

What we can do

"Let no one come to you without leaving better and happier. Be the living expression of God's kindness. Kindness in your face, kindness in your eyes, kindness in your smile."

Mother Teresa

Smile

Smile at everyone you meet.
Smile at those you pass in the street.
Smile at children, dogs.
and especially those who are not smiling back at you.
They need it most of all.

A smile lightens your spirit and makes you happy.
Even if it doesn't change the person you're smiling at, it will eventually change you.
We can't begin to care for each other and help each other if we can't bear to look at one another and connect.

If we are able to look at another human being and see him or her as deserving of love, care, comfort, and happiness, then we are looking at that person through the eyes of God.

When that happens and only when that happens can the world begin to change.

"Nothing is more honorable than a grateful heart."

Seneca

Give Thanks, Say Grace

GRACE

❦

Thank you for the food we eat
Thank you for the world so sweet
Thank you for the birds that sing
Thank you God, for everything

❦

Creator, Earth Mother
we thank you for our lives and this beautiful day.
Thank you for this circle of friends
and the opportunity to be together.
We give thanks to the animals who have given their lives
that we may continue with ours.
Please help us honor them through how we live our lives

God, we thank you for this food
for rest and home and all things good
for wind and rain and sun above
but most of all, for those we love

May the peace and blessing of God
descend upon us as we receive of his bounty
and may our hearts be filled
with love for one another

God, we thank you for all the good things you provide
and we pray for a time when people everywhere shall
have the abundance they need

Amen

Give Thanks, Say Grace

In this world where so many are suffering and starving, the very least we can do is say "grace" before our meals.
We need to give thanks for being blessed to have this food on our table and being able to share it with our loved ones.
We will not go hungry tonight.

Our children will not be among the 25,000 who die each day in this world from hunger and hunger-related disease.
Is that not reason enough to give thanks?

One night, skip dinner.
Give the money you would've spent on dinner to a local food bank or homeless shelter. By bedtime, you'll be hungry.
Like most of the world you'll know what it feels like.
The next day, giving thanks for your food will be much more meaningful to you.
When someone is collecting money for the poor and the hungry, give them as much as you can. **Do not ever turn down an opportunity to give—even if it's only a dollar.**
Giving changes us for the better.

Mother Teresa once said that there are many people who are willing to do big things, but there are few who are willing to do the small things.
Be a person who is willing to do lots of small things. Small efforts by a lot of people can change the world, too.

Helping those less fortunate is one of the things we're on this earth to do. If we don't help each other, who will?

Let Us Be More Than We Have Been

- Say "thank you" with a smile to people who are waiting on you or serving you; that's the least they deserve. Be polite and respectful. It's a tough job.
- Always leave a generous tip. Once in a while, leave a spectacular one!
- Let someone move ahead of you in line.
- Say "please" when asking for something and always smile.
- Treat everyone you meet with respect and kindness.
- Don't talk about people maliciously or participate in gossip.
- Be kind to everyone.
- Let go of old hurts and disagreements.
- When someone tells you something in confidence, keep it confidential.
- Believe that others always have the best of intentions.
- Do something wonderful "anonymously."
- Always give something for a good cause.
- Don't ever ignore someone in need. Do something about it.
- Adopt a homeless pet. It will bring unexpected joy.
- Eat good food, be kind, tell the truth.

"Love begins at home. It's not how much we do, but how much love we put into that action."

Mother Teresa

Make a Loving Home for Your Family

The most important thing you can do
is make your home a sanctuary for your family.

Feather your nest with good food, music, laughter, and bedtime stories.
If your children grow up in an atmosphere of love and gratitude, they will be more able to perpetuate those very things when they are living their own lives.

We need to pass on the love of helping others to our children.
The best way to do it is have them grow up in a home where that exists.
Your family's needs must be met before you venture out into the world to help others.

"Every unfortunate we see is Jesus in disguise"

Mother Teresa

Care

Care enough to act when and where
you see need.
Make it a part of your everyday life.
Get involved—don't just stand there!

- Buy someone a hot meal if they're hungry.
- Help someone to cross the street.
- Offer to carry a heavy bag for someone who is struggling.
- Hold the door for someone behind you or coming toward you.
- Put some money in every charitable collection.
- Open your heart to a person who needs help.
- If you see someone without a coat, get one at Goodwill or take him or her to a shelter.
- Don't judge—care!

When you care, you will act. When you care enough to see all the need in this world, your heart will open and you will feel more love and gratitude for your life and all your blessings. It is then you will have infinitely more to give to those in need.

"If you have men who will exclude any of God's creatures from the shelter of compassion and pity, you will have men who will deal likewise with their fellow men."

St. Francis of Assisi

THE TREE OF LOVE

Embrace All God's Creatures

While human life is the focus of the
Tree of Love plan,
we must also include God's little creatures—
birds, animals, and our pets.
Do what you can for these gentle little souls.
Have water and seed available for the birds
all year, and
provide them with some shelter from storms and
a house for them to use to nest in the spring.
Not only will you be helping them and the
environment, but you will experience great joy
watching them all year at your feeders.
Right now, I'm looking at a downy woodpecker
eat suet and berries from a hollowed-out log on
my bird feeder.
Treat your own pets with the same love and care
you give to the rest
of the family.
They are a part of your life and your family, and
they give so much to us.
They are what we aspire to be—loving,
accepting, forgiving, and always living
in the moment.
We can learn a lot from them.

EMBRACE ALL GOD'S CREATURES

God created them for us, to be companions and to love us and enrich our lives. They give us all their love. We owe them some of ours.

Love

We have so much more love inside than we know.
The only way to find it is to give it away.
In doing so, we create even more.
The gift of love is the greatest of all.
If we can love each other, then all things become possible.
Love can open our hearts and minds.
Love helps us grow in wisdom and compassion for others.
Love helps us to accept our differences and look past imperfections.

Love is the only thing that can truly change the world,
because it is the only thing that can truly change us.

*"If you can't feed a hundred people,
then feed just one."*

Mother Teresa

Be Grateful You Are Able to Help

Being able to bring comfort to others is a great blessing.
Nothing is more frustrating than seeing need or suffering
and not being able to do something to help.

*When we help others we are achieving our higher
purpose.
We are connecting with the possibility that we can
be more than we have been.*

Reach out to the elderly, the poor, sick, and the lonely
wherever you find them.
Chances are they have no one to make their day brighter.
Read to them; spend some time with them.
Take them a little treat or something to brighten their day.

*In helping each other, we are serving God. Let us
remember that and be grateful for the opportunity.*

"A meal prepared with love feeds the spirit as well as the body."

Mother Teresa

Nurture

When you visit someone who is alone,
take something that you have prepared for him or her.
They will see it for what it is: a gift of love and caring.

What it is doesn't matter.
What it will do for the person receiving it does matter.
Preparing food for someone is an act of love and nurturing.
When you feed the hungry, you are also feeding the
emptiness that may be inside of them.

*The important thing is to do everything
with love.
Even the smallest bit of food becomes a feast for the
soul when it is prepared and offered with love.*

*"We need to find God
and he cannot be found
in noise
and restlessness.
God is the friend of silence.
See how nature—trees, flowers,
grass—grows in silence.
See the stars, the moon and the sun,
how they move in silence.
We need silence
to be able to touch souls."*

Mother Teresa

Pray for Guidance and Strength

If we are committed to helping others,
we must pray for guidance and strength.
God will give us whatever we need to
accomplish this work.
We need only to listen for his voice.
We'll find it in the silence of prayer or meditation.

*We must know that what we are trying to
accomplish will not be easy.
If it were easy, it would already be done.*

With God's strength and guidance, it will be possible.
We are God's humble servants, and we are choosing to
serve our fellow man.
We do not come to this task with pride or for our own
gratification, but with a willingness to let go of self.
In doing so, we are able to do all that is required with love
and compassion and humble hearts.

"May God give back to you in love all the love and all the joy and peace you have sown around you, all over the world."

Mother Teresa

Bring Joy to Those You Help

Joy can be found everywhere, in all things.
Unfortunately, some cannot see it.
It's important to have joy in your life and in your heart
and bring it to the lives of others.

Without joy, one cannot truly experience all
this life has to offer.

Allow yourself to feel the joy you bring to
a person who needs comfort.
You are helping that person experience one of
God's greatest gifts.

*Make it your intention to wrap everything you do
in joy. It will change you and the lives of
all those you touch.*

Inspiration

In order to accomplish the great task we have agreed to accept, we will need inspiration and encouragement.

I have included some prayers and quotes from
Mother Teresa and St. Francis of Assisi.
These are my favorites and they inspire me to be a better person and do a better job.
I hope they inspire you, as well.

They devoted their hearts and their lives to helping the poor, loving the unloved, and feeding the hungry.

Read these prayers when you need a reminder of what we're trying to accomplish.
Their words will be a source of comfort and encouragement to you.

THE TREE OF LOVE

Mother Teresa

We were blessed to have Mother Teresa working
in this world until 1997.
She founded the Missionaries of Charity in 1950, and
she devoted the rest of her life to loving and caring for
the poor, the sick, the homeless, the orphaned, and the
dying. There was no cause that was hopeless to her. Mother
worked with lepers and those who had AIDS. She made
sure that at the end of their lives, they had love and care
and a peaceful death.

In 1979 she was awarded the Nobel Peace Prize for her
work. Pope John Paul II took the unusual step of declaring
her beatification only a few years after her death.

She is now known as "Blessed Teresa of Calcutta." Her
message of love lives, and her work must continue through
all of us who are dedicated to the principle of caring for all
human beings.

"I'm not exactly sure what heaven will be like, but I know that when we die and it comes time for God to judge us he will not ask, 'How many good things have you done in your life?'
He will ask, 'How much love did you put into what you did?'"

Mother Teresa

THE TREE OF LOVE

Prayers and Quotes of Mother Teresa

"Make us worthy Lord, to serve our fellow man
throughout the world who live and die in
poverty and hunger.
Give them, through our hands, their daily bread,
and by our understanding, give love, peace, and joy."

*"If we have no peace, it is because we have forgotten
that we belong to each other."*

*"Kindness is a language we all understand.
Even the blind can see it
and the deaf can hear it ."*

Mother Teresa

*"If we pray, we will believe.
If we believe, we will love.
If we love, we will serve."*

*"The fruit of silence is prayer.
The fruit of prayer is faith.
The fruit of faith is love.
The fruit of love is service.
The fruit of service is peace."*

Mother Teresa

THE TREE OF LOVE

"Do not think that love in order to be genuine has to be extraordinary. What we need is to love without getting tired. Be faithful in small things, for it is in them that your strength lies."

"Being unwanted, unloved, uncared for, forgotten by everybody, I think that is a much greater hunger, a much greater poverty than the person who has nothing to eat."

Mother Teresa

St. Francis of Assisi

We know a lot of the work of Mother Teresa because she was a contemporary. St. Francis lived one thousand years ago. He is the patron saint of animals, birds, and the environment. He was definitely a man ahead of his time.

Animals have always found a protector in St. Francis. Early legends speak of his love for animals and his gentle nature. He once referred to the birds as his "little brethren" because they would flock to the roadside where he was preaching near Bevagna. He found inspiration in every sunrise, in flowers, streams, forests, birds, and all God's creatures. He once asked a village to feed a wolf because the wolf had attacked the villager's sheep. St. Francis felt that "Brother Wolf" was hungry and that's why he ate the sheep. So, the villagers fed the wolf and the attacks stopped. St. Francis loved animals because in their innocent, loving presence he sensed the presence of God. He was a man full of love for his fellow man, animals, and all of nature. In his mind, we were all one in the eyes of God. I have always felt a kinship with St. Francis, even before I knew much about him. At least now I know why.

The Prayer of St. Francis

Lord, make me an instrument of thy peace.
Where there is hatred, let me sow love.
Where there is injury, pardon.
Where there is doubt, faith.
Where there is despair, hope
Where there is darkness, light, and
Where there is sadness, joy.
Grant that I may not so much
seek to be consoled as to console;
To be understood, as to understand;
To be loved, as to love;
For it is giving that we receive.
It is in pardoning that we are pardoned
It is in dying that we are born to eternal life.

The Tree of Love

ST. FRANCIS OF ASSISI

The Tree of Love its roots hath spread
Deep in my heart, and rears its head;
Rich are its fruits; they joy dispense;
Transport the heart, and ravish sense.
In love's sweet swoon, to thee I cleave,
    Bless'd source of love.

Take the Pledge

THE TREE OF LOVE PLEDGE

I believe in the principles of love, caring, and comfort.
I believe that my participation in creating that love,
caring, and comfort in my own life, with my loved
ones and others I know, can be the beginning of a new
world for mankind.

If we, as women, pledge to begin this undertaking
and help guide others who wish to participate, then
we are the architects who will help bring about the
change we all want to see in the world.
We will all be a part of it.

"Start by doing what is necessary; then do what's possible;
and suddenly you are doing the impossible."
St. Francis of Assisi

I pledge my gifts as a woman, my ability to love and
nurture and comfort, to those in my circle of friends and

family and to do the same for all those in need, to the best of my ability. I vow to encourage everyone I know to do the same, until this world has been forever changed by our love.

signed and dated: _____

Food for Thought

THE TREE OF LOVE

We have so much.

We have multiple houses,
multiple cars, jewelry,
ridiculous amounts of designer clothing, and
tons of other material possessions that
we can never fully use.

Let's take a quick look at how we are living.
What are the necessities of life?

Obviously, there is food, clothing, shelter.

But how much is enough?

How much food is in your refrigerator right now that is
spoiling and will be thrown away in the garbage?
How much do you estimate you have thrown away over
the last year? Five years? Ten years?
How many clothes are hanging in your closets right now or
stored in boxes in your basement that you will never
wear again?
How many toys are strewn about in your garage or
basement that your children have outgrown
or lost interest in?

FOOD FOR THOUGHT

"Live simply, so that others may simply live."

Mother Teresa

THE TREE OF LOVE

Take an inventory of your life.

Get rid of what you don't need—and don't replace it!
Donate clothing and coats to a shelter or Goodwill.
Plan menus to use leftovers so you don't waste
so much food.

Be aware of your actions in the future.
Be embarrassed by your excess in the past.

If we live more simply, it will give us more time to be of
service to others who truly need our help

FOOD FOR THOUGHT

Be Mindful

Smile at a stranger and say "Hello"

Donate to any good cause

Be silent for ten minutes a day
(so that your heart may hear more clearly)

Take a moment to breathe in fresh air and listen
to the wind

Watch the birds come and go from their feeders

Smell the rain in the air before a storm

Tell your husband and children you love them—every day

Prepare a meal with love and say grace

Comfort your children; make them feel loved

Care about everything

Help whenever you can

Be grateful for your life and blessings

THE TREE OF LOVE

Be kind to all God's creatures

Be optimistic and cheerful

Don't be petty

Be generous with your heart, your time, and your words

and most importantly

Offer up all your efforts to God

Here are a few suggestions for National Charities.
There are many more, and there are many local charities:

Save the Children
savethechildren.org
1-800-728-3843

Salvation Army
www.salvationarmyusa.com

St Judes Children's Research Hospital
www.stjude.org

THE TREE OF LOVE

Global Hunger Project
(p) 212-251-9100

National Alliance to End Hunger
(p) 202-638-1526

The Sunshine Foundation
helps fulfill the dreams of terminally ill children ages 3–18
www.sunshinefoundation.org

American Bird Conservancy
contact 888-247-3624

American Red Cross
1-800-HELPNOW (435-7669)

Animal Welfare Institute
awionline.org

See their websites for more information

The Tree of Love Workbook Pages

Profile Work Sheets
(Fill out these sheets when determining
who you want to help and how)

Tree of Love Meeting Notes
(Fill out meeting forms when you assist women
in deciding who they wish to help and how)

Things to Do

Local Charities
(Make notes on local charities
for which you may volunteer)

Notes

Profile Sheets

Name_____

Age_____

Address_____
_____

Phone_____

Email_____

Relationship_____

Action needed_____
_____
_____
_____

Action taken_____
_____
_____
_____

Follow-up_____
_____

Comments_____
_____

THE TREE OF LOVE

Profile Sheets

Name_____

Age_____

Address_____

_____

Phone_____

Email_____

Relationship_____

Action needed_____

_____

_____

_____

Action taken_____

_____

_____

_____

Follow-up_____

_____

Comments_____

_____

PROFILE SHEETS

Profile Sheets

Name_____

Age_____

Address_____

_____

Phone_____

Email_____

Relationship_____

Action needed_____

_____

_____

_____

Action taken_____

_____

_____

_____

Follow-up_____

_____

Comments_____

_____

THE TREE OF LOVE

Profile Sheets

Name_____

Age_____

Address_____

_____

Phone_____

Email_____

Relationship_____

Action needed_____

_____

_____

_____

Action taken_____

_____

_____

_____

Follow-up_____

_____

Comments_____

_____

Profile Sheets

Name_____

Age_____

Address_____

_____

Phone_____

Email_____

Relationship_____

Action needed_____

_____

_____

_____

Action taken_____

_____

_____

_____

Follow-up_____

_____

Comments_____

_____

THE TREE OF LOVE

Profile Sheets

Name_____

Age_____

Address_____

_____

Phone_____

Email_____

Relationship_____

Action needed_____

_____

_____

_____

Action taken_____

_____

_____

_____

Follow-up_____

_____

Comments_____

_____

PROFILE SHEETS

Things to Do

Things to Do

Local Charities

Name of organization

Address

Phone

Need volunteers?

What I can do

Name of organization

Address

Phone

Need volunteers?

What can I do

Name of organization

Address

Phone

Need volunteers?

What can I do?

NOTES

Notes

NOTES

Notes

Notes

Tree of Love Meeting

Date:

In attendance: _____

Plans designed for attendee relative and friends:

1.

2.

3.

4.

5.

6.

Follow-up needed:

NOTES

We want to hear from you.

Let us know your stories.
What strategies are working?
How have you changed lives for the better?
What have you learned about yourself?
Do you have any insights to share with your other
"Tree of Love" participants?

Log on to our website:
www.thetreeofloveplan.com

Register and be counted.
Share your experiences with us on our blog
and on Facebook

Made in the USA
Middletown, DE
02 May 2016